Unraveling the Nightshade Labyrinth

Unraveling the Nightshade Labyrinth

Lindsay Warhusrt

WALNUT STREET
—**PUBLISHING**—

ISBN: 978-1-967230-05-1

Walnut Street Publishing
1673 South Holtzclaw Studio 14
Chattanooga, TN 37404
www.walnutstreetpublishing.com

for us, mostly

book of contents

introduction

Nightshade, known to scientists as "Solanaceae", is a plant family that contains both potatoes, eggplants, and chili peppers; yet it is best known for its poisonous properties. The uncertain etymology of the Latin name roughly translates to both "soothe" and "sun"- very different connotations than those typically imputed to nightshade!

Interestingly enough, nightshade can be used as a pharmaceutical as well as for self-destruction. It also has roots in nicotine and cocaine, making it an addictive substance. If improperly digested, nightshade can cause hallucinations, pupil dilation, cessation of heartbeat, involuntary muteness, and death.

Partake at your own risk.

This book is a labyrinth, not a maze. What is the difference, you ask? A maze, much like life, has many choices; many deviant ways to many disparate endings. The choices that you make in a maze all lead you to some sort of exit.

A labyrinth, on the other hand, has only one predetermined path that you must travel in order to resolve it and find yourself blinking in the daylight. The path through this narrative has been plotted for you.

Enter at your own risk.

I: the nightshade (2022)

"Again and again, this constant forsaking."

-          Natasha Trethewey, "Myth", Native Guard

"In this country, {he} doesn't know
the word for "drowning" and yells:
"I am diving for the last time!""
-     Ilya Kaminsky, "For His Wife", *Deaf Republic*

we start with a swan song

"you are too young to be this angry" - listen.

under my furtive fingertips,
every shade of serendipity brushes off
and precipices of consciousness
collapse into the wine-dark sea

when i baptise my torn knees in the kitchen sink.

listen.
parented by motherboards, soldered together
by apathy, crossed wires stripped by controversy,
you will hear
the over-fertilised voice of a sporadic generation, planting beautiful things

and

ripping them up when they do not grow fast enough...
an ecosystem of immediate gratification; blue in the mesmeric glow of
their own incipient discontent.
i know because i am one of them-
my hot head overridden
by their cold feet.

listen.
next time you are forsaken in the terminal,
ask yourself why
the american dream has always been to leave america.
where do you think you are going?

listen.

we are a starving planet circling a dying star
and i am writing poems about someone
who will not translate them: my gesticulation, intense,
mistaken for violence in another tongue.

listen.

we could not differentiate between a firecracker and a gunshot,
but we were all celebrating a life we did not have to live,
a death we did not have to touch
to be responsible for-

if your age has not infuriated you,
i envy you the privilege of that insulating ignorance.

listen closely enough and you will understand why
home is a curse word in my mouth.

re: surface tension

tonight is
one of those nights where i'd like
to float to the top of that ultramarine sea
without a shore that inhabits
your lovely unfathomable mind

and be back, unreachably deep,
by morning.

but beneath my knife-punctured back, creatures
that have never seen the moon would rise
up to the surface and reflect
her in trailing phosphorus,
reaching tendrils, tentacles,
to gently pull
me back where i belong-

deep in the darkest recesses of your mind,
beside every other memory you refuse to let breathe
for fear the oxygen transcribes them
into something like guilt.

say it with what's left of your chest

i don't
hate my body
except
the parts
that look like
they are
mine

just listen to people
for fun.
when they laugh,
they leave unspoken
cruelty;
giving back what is
within the echo

no vacancy

hannah once told me
that tears are good for your skin;
if you rub them in well they'll cleanse you. lord,
i'm sick of grief being given a purpose-
perhaps if we stopped furnishing the hollows beneath our clavicle, sorrow
would find itself a more comfortable dwelling.

between the interim and the aftermath

all my memories of him are lodged in places i cannot stay:
the crosswalk; the stairwell; the thin places;
the unresolved interval dissipating into dissonance on the organ called a
heart; the month of may;

but i pause here- equidistant from the future and the past, a blind woman
closing her eyes- expecting him to re-enter
without an invitation.
the sun stretches out on the wall
but never snaps;

i watch it creep laps as i suspend myself.

and i tore out the center of this poem with my teeth. because
none of these words translate into an apology
for being the sort of woman who, in order to catch a wave, will stand in
deserts and pray for tsunamis.

stay, i wanted to say- stay.
but i tie myself up with syntax and gag myself on inflections
with my attempts to lodge in all the places i cannot stay-
the only person i've ever known how to be is someone
who speaks too often and still manages
to say very little.

bone appetite

there came a day when
my teeth were no longer the only bones left uncovered.

this was when the anorexia was still in his pointing fingers;
but long after
it was crouching in my rib cage,
and long before
the handprints around my throat migrated
to collarbones, wrists, thighs.
in those days,
nothing i did was palatable.
all my table manners were revolting,
he said, all the food i'm relearning to love
was thickening my distasteful body.

(how could you not lose your appetite? seeing me carved open, devouring
my own flesh?)

it's still true, to this day;
i'll cut myself into bite-sized morsels
for anyone, i'll serve myself up and i still
am not enough to satisfy because
it's me, it's me, no matter
how raw or cooked or kosher or seasoned-
it's still flavored like me,
still tastes like the poisons we've been devouring our whole lives. it's a
family recipe we followed, starved for affection.

(sorry about the teeth marks, he said: i thought showing love meant
inflicting pain.)

to the bone:
that is how we love in my house.
eating and being eaten.

(the difference between us, my brother, was that you were eating me alive
and i, i was feeling guilty
for making you sick.)

entropy

you've been left clinging to the wreckage of it   all

snarled sails, splintered mast, lonely and useless   things

tell me, why do you need   that

life? like the tide, it will go and   come

we can only face it   together

in truth, we   must

learn to ride waves so we know how to   fall

like our loneliness- we'll drown if we swim   apart

preacher's daughter
(for o.)

she doesn't understand   what the rest of us see
anything perfect is   clearly
only perfect because it   is the future; and the past
has not yet been   held against us-
loved.   without merit.

we are homesick for a place we've never called home
(a sonnet)

reveal yourself to me, new york; display
chimera corporeal, dreams concrete.
within subways, the exhortations sound
to mind the gap between. am i unclear?
in brooklyn, boulevards of thought traverse
past doors that sharpened mind left locked,
enigma cracking under torpid stares.
inform the shelf memoirs have bowed that i
am here to read; to find the secret life;
devour; in short, internalize new york.

the volta here, fulcrum, the turn, the crux:
to me, new york, you are a nom de plume-
pursued because enigma beckons still.
explain yourself to me. am i unclear?

tenebrism

october- so the naked tree branches score a sky
already bleached, older than bones; another woman
with an intense capacity for secrets.

i ask this sky for answers and god sends me a thunderstorm.

perhaps i have not suffered as others have,
but the roots of my unshivering grief
have been watered.

then the sunlight sharpens against the piano keys;
his hair tapers into the back of his neck
with a gracefulness that makes me catch my breath;
a turn of the head as a twist of the knife; a poignancy that parallels pain
as honey drips down my hand....
and the ache in my throat multiplies into something very like laughter.

oh, life,
i could forgive you anything
save for being so hauntingly lovely.

sometimes there are guard rails; sometimes there are ghosts

you are one patch of november ice and two lungfuls of paramedic air
away
from a flatline; and i'd pay my respects, but i resent the implication that
i owe you anything.

at this distance, across the chapel, my focus falls on
the whisper of scripture's pages like rain on window panes
and your guilty tobacco-scented hands restless in your lap as the offering
plate, followed by communion, passes you by;
those hemlock eyes sharpened with the overwhelming clarity
of someone who wants to disappear.

this yearning expands when it is cornered.
you are two mourners and one coffin away
from interring whatever remains of yourself.

i drew labyrinths around you to understand your wandering
while you gave my sorrow new mazes to solve-
for that, at least,
i can thank you.

the tide from which we come; the tide to which we must return

I.
i am shaped like the parabola that a finger embosses
into the upper palm
(the end parenthesis of an irrelevant afterthought)
but i am not the moon-
what the tides have washed away from me will always come back
changed;
twice left, once returned.
if we were a shape,
we'd be a ray
("the ray that runs from the point of tangency")
it has a beginning, my love,
but it is never ending.
but we are not the sun-
what light we cast only seemed brilliant to me because i was accustomed
to blindness.

II.
what is the point?

it's one of those things, you know, imagining my fingertips coursing
down your spine; the crevasse in your chest;
the promontory of the collarbones; over
the senseless delicacy of your craggy profile; the long legs
initialed with the name of a reckless childhood;
over all your delft blue postage stamp tattoos
from places you were never delivered;
these questing fingertips summiting the ridges of your shoulders,
callusing your breathing.
i tell you where it hurts, and you put both sets of hands
over the edges of the wound,
bringing them back together.

for long enough. for long enough.

in reality,
your fingers are heat-seeking missiles; my body
a white flag, camouflaged in bedsheets. you put your knuckles
to my jaw, a fist to my missing rib;

you do not ask me who was taken from me; do not tell me
that my brittle crystalline eyes could make a drowning man beg for
water.
bodies of water against forms of stone; hurled
against the cliff sides of you, again and again,
seeking any grasp; any crevasse to pour myself into-

you have always been the point against which I must break, you know,
you know.

you know how it goes.

if you can't have what you want, you take what you can get;
knowing you won't make it to shore won't stop you
from swimming for the cliffs.

III.
you claim you are afraid to capsize,
 but you think of drowning the way
you think of oxygen-

that is to say: constantly, and never at all

II: the labyrinth (2023)

"What is truth, anyway?
And isn't everything fiction in the end,

an interfusion of myths?...

...there were questions that hollowed out deep galleries in him, forming

as it were a labyrinth..."

-    Camille De Toledo, Theseus

"Terrible things breed in broken hearts... it cannot be long before her
grief turns, as grief always does, to rage."

-    Euripedes, "Medea"

ménagerie d'melancolie

anyways, i
hope you're well.
        i'm about the same, you
                            know how i get, my
        imbalanced brain
        up
filling
            tipping o
                        v
                            e

                                r

            spilling things intended to be vesseled

            "why does it affect you
differently from everyone?"
(my animal trainer asks patiently).

                i don't know, grandmaster;
            perhaps we all felt this way in the cage.
perhaps i was enclosed within a mind
            that equates deprivation with depth.

perhaps everyone else
                            was just better at

    convincing themselves they were not captive
                            to their own sorrows.

on rocking a sinking ship

I: *brooklyn*
new york overheard it first; my clouded breath as evident in the chilly air
as the falsity interred in my inflection
as i protest to my friends: "but i am not an angry person!"
and all five of us laughed; i and they and every place i have ever walked
away from; i and they and the diaspora of past selves;
the flat tonal chuckle
of those who are not deceived.

no one else in the subway found our irony amusing.

II: *tennessee*
take politics and religion off the table.
let's bring power to dinner instead
and if we talk long enough about him,
politics and religion will take of their masks, slide out the chairs,
and take their place among us-
which is to say:
above.

there's no heart of gold that cannot be bought by a silver tongue.
they can sell us anything
but they cannot explain how it holds its value.

III: *tennessee again*
at my parent's church, someone threw a dart barbed
like "welcome home" and popped my rubber smile. i
caught the turn of phrase
between the same teeth that mouth the national
anthem without tasting it:

this annotated smile, reflexive,
wider than the distance between us. you turn in a hall
of mirrors and are brought back up
against your own falsity.

can you trust a home built by a carnival of illusionists?
is my escape luck of the draw, or did i learn to play a
bad hand well? can we call it magic
if it's just a trick?

let me ask it this way: was what you saw on my face a
smirk or a flinch?

IV: tennessee, still
oh, america,
you flimsical republic of single-use travesties-
you'd think we like being out of control
the way we let ourselves spin out;
but we discard the solution before we study
the problem, hit the brakes before the key
has even turned-
lord,
i worry that we'll get nowhere.

V. *still tennessee*
do you believe in anything? can you prove your
dendrochronology bears truth? we have less rings than
saturn; our youth evident to any who can number
them. on our self-transcribed axis, we spiral in, and in,
and in,
and in.

VI: *still tennessee, but further south*
we can be called witnesses, but we cannot answer to our crimes.
where do you think we are going?

VII. *what is known as "the volunteer state"*
when i'm in tennessee,
i say "fuck" like i know what it means.
"our fatherland, who art in heaven-" you flinch, our mother tongue forced
in your mouth-
and we keep watching the news of a country
that we no longer bear any resemblance to.

this much i know to be true of parents and homelands:
if we did not choose them purposefully
we will not return to them deliberately.

you never want to be a father;
you never asked to be a son.

part I: the icarus cycle
(for r.m.h)

what a lot of love there must be in here
if locks that put names to it
can nearly collapse a bridge in paris.

what a lot of love there must be in me
if i can, unflinching, sluice your blood off a patio
so our younger brother doesn't have to
circumnavigate it.

this is not the sort of house
in which one imagines ghosts, but what are we
if not haunted?

and i am trying not to understand
that you leapt from the window
perpendicular to the one i closed
when i erased the first draft of my suicide note-
when i resolved to let the unlivable thing within me survive-

of such moments a life is made.

and i'm well aware
that i'm merely trying to unravel
my own charred bridges of harm; to exorcize the
inherent terror of what my parents built...
whatever is drafted by architects
full of rage with death contracts left unsigned...

but i hope you believed
that what you were killing was not yourself,
but something monstrous inside you.

there was love, there within you, too.
it deserved to survive this horror.

aren't we lucky that it did?

part II: the daedalus cycle

he says,

"you are too young to know what love means."

and this from him- who removed the wings from a
social butterfly to pin to his framed ambitions.

a beat too late, i retort:
"you are too old to be this hateful."

and this from me- who brings a bleeding pen to every clean slate;
teeth sharpened from the rougher edges
of my own sentences; dogmatism bitten off ragged
between them. but still.

i will not be the one to drag my rage seven times
around the walls of this labyrinth
until it is whittled into something better known as grief.
strong enough to hold on, weak enough
to never let it go:

he might be my older brother
but i have always been the bigger man.

oracle condemns delphi

splinteringly infinite
complex inner mythology,
unweave me and rethread the labyrinth
deep in my head
where the minotaur rests,
where the hunger is:

if i will be his voice, he swears to be the mouth that contains me.

that mouth:
always hungry, ever feeding,
splitting the bones and lapping the blood;
and tantalus; immolation, κυρία κυρία;
and sisyphus; cyclical, repetitive;
and the styx churns the river wheel, ferries the same souls;
and the eagle devours the liver
it must have grown sick of eating centuries ago-
tired of the taste of man
tired of the lack of rot
tired of the endless repetition.

it seems to me
the worst punishment gods can conjure is to be
never-ending; never-changing;
an existence that continues and continues and never
ceases to be.

«καμίλα»

if a child is flung over a river, tied to a javelin to escape a war,
at what point do the weapon and the girl become one?

if the battle is to the death,
how can this killing thing be an instrument of life?

 war was not my first language;
but family lines, cut too short to be considered ties, taught me
that persuasion orates best with a blade between its teeth-

that's what it is to use one word to mean two things. to use that blade
intended for the battlefield
to transplant any limb that reaches for violence.

don't you know that poisoned fruit growing from a rotten family tree dies
as it destroys?
don't you know that i will swear my loyalty to anything
that i will not survive?

that's what it is
to know two languages and mean something untranslatable:

i tell you plainly
that i will outlive this
outrage.

further down and farther out
erasure of "heavier" by odesza & yellow house

hemlock   fingers
bending and breaking   light
pristine, deftly moving   to hide   you

aching
in your nightshade
labyrinth of desire

dislocation
(for j.r.c.g.)

you said to call me when i got home.

maybe i'll do that in a few years
when i actually feel like i've found home, mom.
when i'm finally bigger than the town that raised me.
 where do you think i am going?

it was home- but it was my parent's house, but it was a dorm room, but it
was his arms, but it was a friend's couch, but now i'm paying rent, mother,
i'm doing laundry, there are less poems and more grocery lists; home is
just another place to run away from;
everything has changed and nothing at all is different
because i'm still not certain
where i belong.

it was never the answer
and ever the question-
it's just a concept i'm trying to bury in words
so i can take it like a pill or a shot,
take it like a doctors' appointment or a house party- a little too loud and
a little too quick,
you understand, to cover the nerves and coat the throat-
questionable, unanswerable, mother,

click your ruby lips together three times until
they tell me where to go.

this i swear to you:
wherever i am going, i will not need an answering machine.
and when i finally return your call,
listen for the silence.
it will tell you i've found the hardest place to leave.

august
(for m.b.f.)

the sky is pregnant with
storms, an inevitable landfall of
pewter, charcoal,
swirling like the underside of a wave or a
van gogh in grayscale- upset,
close to the end, on the
verge of breaking down.

in the poolside cypresses, cryptic without meaning anything at all,
the cicadas protest.

summer
is already planning a wake- the funeral
dirges chanted by
the same insects that
sang her birthday anthem

but i,
ears underwater and eyes
fixed on the faithless roiling clouds
am not listening for anything in particular
anyone in particular
except my own belated
revelations-

august does not take her time with us anymore
because anything will kill you if you give it long enough.

and what if we outlive ourselves?
what then?

predator

call a man a monster
and statues are erected in his honor.
call a woman a liar
and the coin is forgotten between roof of mouth and hollow of jawbone.

for every two promises kept, the price is one lie.
fire speaks in tongues of its own-
what need had you for mine?

do you trust me?
do you think i tell the myth aright?
with my mother tongue cut out and the glow of your invading ships
behind me?
go on, eat my liver. tomorrow i'll grow a new one.

a man is still a man is still an animal-
one way or another he'll take the heart;
perhaps with his smile, perhaps with his teeth-

but i am not like him.
i do not have to have him between my canines
to identify his appetites.
i have been prey for too long
to misunderstand the palate of a predator.

do you trust me?
do you think i tell the myth aright?
do you believe the one dressed like you,
or this black sheep of a girl who decries him 'wolf'?
go on. treat him like he can be tamed. in the afterglow,
he will be pawing at your door.

god save the sinner, and god spare the saint

(for c.m.s.)
the pharisee says the joan-of-arc bob sets off my god complex
sneers built into the apse of his throat.
"if suffering makes you sacred," he mocks, "shouldn't you be better by
now?"

shouldn't i?

all that's left to be
is the crossing guard; guardian of the crucifix;
heaven-sent and hell-bent;
patron saint of the unorthodox pedestrian and the heretic jaywalker alike.
the passers-by will genuflect as they navigate
the stations of the crosswalk. i will be canonised
in street signs and prophesied by half-glimpsed roadkill,
my hagiography mourned and forgotten
by the time the clover-leaf intersection swallows my part-time disciples
and spits them out onto another interstate:

this is my body, broken for you.

must we always be martyrs to our future?

a savior trades his crown of thorns for barbed wire around a mission;

blind men beg for sight only to pluck out their own stained-glass eyes; and

all the angels round the throne cry out:

"if suffering makes you sacred,

then jesus,shouldn't i be better by now?"

shouldn't we all?

litany against three men

it was	your anger against me
my body first	and then the space
you had	made for it
no	room
right	inside
to enter	my snarling mouth

what is your only comfort in life and death?

when he told us to be fishers of men,
i didn't know he intended me to watch the sunrise
on the third day
next to the body i dragged from the same river i was baptized in. the flat
sparkle of the water unbothered by another fatality,
earth already clinging to your corpse
as if it cannot wait to consume you.
from it you were taken,
to it you must return.

we were both looking for jesus in that water.
was all you saw your reflection?

in your wake,
they'll tell me that somehow it makes me better than you
that i drink wine to be saved and you drank it to be damned-
a libation swallowed by this once damable water.

we were both on our knees.
to whom were you praying?

your story was a tragedy and mine is a myth
yet the same author that hurried you to your unhappily ever after
is still turning pages full of me; still letting me vomit lake water and words.
my first poem was a suicide note.
my existence encapsulated in the pills shrouded beneath my childhood
mattress.
amen. hallelujah. it is finished.
(it was not.)

we were both in your afterword.
can you guess which of us was alive to read it?

who were you?
why were you?
may the fates be damned:
what could someone like me have said
to give you a different ending?
to diverge this river from the path it was ordained to traverse?

III: the unraveling (2024)

"And they said, "Look, Lord, here are two swords." And he said to them, "It is enough."
> - Luke 22:38

"Let no one mistake us for the fruit of violence- but that violence, having passed through the fruit, failed to spoil it."

> - Ocean Vuong, *On Earth We're Briefly Gorgeous*

the book of job

"Have you ever given orders to the morning, or shown the dawn its place, that it might take the earth by the edges and shake the wicked out of it?"
- *Job 38:12-13*

awe and i do not often cross paths-
we do not intersect like the hawk
that arrowed from the sky,
splitting my morning into shivering halves,
a single sparrow in his sights.

if i were superstitious, my widening eyes
would have read it as an omen.

instead,
i put a hand over the mouth that called God to bear witness.

empires rise and fall;
gods forget and are forgiven;
the Reaper unsheathes the scythe, hungry for his gleaning of the
harvest; but the Gardener's hand does not flinch-
and the sparrow shudders free
and the enemy soars back defeated-

awe finds me empty and fills me to the brim.

excused absences from the bird sanctuary

(for M.A.W.)

"riddle me this:
can you differentiate between
a girl who runs away from home
and a crop-winged finch
who stays in the aviary?"

the girl has a ready rage for a steady stage.

"and the other?"

the bird was the ready stage for the steady rage.

(to be angry, she had to survive-
I had to be angry to survive.

do you understand the difference now?)

"But the fighter still remains"

(after "The Boxer" by Simon and Garfunkel)

Did you think knuckles like these are spawned by sporadic boxing
sessions on unclaimable Tuesdays? Let me show you
how I used to curl my fingertips into the hinges of every door I thought
you'd leave me by so I could feel your desertions twice.
Let me introduce you to old grief
when it reenters with new faces. Let me demonstrate
why there are claw marks on the surface of everything I've ever loved.

Do you find it childish?
Four layers of paint deep and you will hit skin: at heart, I am still the age
I was when the first lights flickered and the rooms were
rumored to be haunted. Even then,
 I was old enough to understand that once you learn how to leave,
nothing can teach you to stay. Sometimes you return
only to remember why you left in the first place...

It is not always beautiful, being a tourist attraction.
It is not always beautiful being a tourist attraction
and nobody's home.

Nobody's home. I am growing tired
of shadowboxing against the boarded-up back door of your heart.

Nobody's home. My fists are my own again
when they forget
where they wanted to belong; when they remember why they left in the
first place.

Nobody's home. I will not keep defending the places that abandoned me.

I didn't want to forgive you so I never asked you to apologize

Fourteen years later, and I am still trying
to understand how the fragile star-shaped flowers outside Zion canyon
survived the temperature of that unforgiving April. It was our first and last
time there.
Mostly, I remember
the bone-chilling xeric bite of it all; but I also recall
the feeling of adulthood that is only achieved by walking,
 alone,
a long distance to a camp restroom; I do remember
spooling between the cave dwellings... how difficult it was for me
to turn my head up toward them, the thick scarf at my adolescent neck
impeding my eye's progress.
Oh, the stars out there. I don't recall those daughtering stars
but I can still imagine the second-hand telescope tilted towards them
mirroring the angle of my father's pointing finger when he gestured to
the striations of a canyon wall, fault lines; all broken and yet still holding
itself together. That apex in my vision was the inverse of the slope I
slithered down, iced fingertips locating a new type of pain: the stunted,
serrated chip of rock I would pocket
with two types of limestone in it. Colors like turmeric and cinnamon.

Caught between two immensities, canyon and crumb,
he knelt there with me
and marveled.

You can call me my father's daughter
in the same way you call a snowbird after what they seek to avoid,
but everything I know about Zane Grey and
building campfires that stay alight and being 1/64th Mohican, I know
because of him.

Fireweed

(for T.M.K.)

Will you let it make you brutal
to thrive in cruel places? In the aftermath?
I'll fill in the gaps; I'll embrace the scorched earth.
I'll be the first to move when the world stills.
Let me be your Atlas
if there's a sky that needs shouldering
or a homeland that needs discovering.

If nothing gold can stay, let me be the green
that cobbles the forest's footprint.

I am not very good, darling,
but I'm better than I was raised to be.
Grown from a twisted family tree,
transplanted, pruned by kinder hands than
those that earthed me-
if my rotten fruit can offer some nourishment, I'll grow as well as I can.

If I cannot be the fire, if I may not be the light,
may I be the one
who makes the burnt places
habitable.

Every Member of the Circle Has Their Own Angle

Max says the pine tree that grew him
was his mythology,
though the science in his synapses
disregards the existence of a soul.

How can you suppress a myth into paper?
Is the release form printed on it
a poem to the death of a pantheon
or an ode to the wine-dark nymph
that grew too comprehensive and had to be
chopped down to size?

Once a forest, now a fire.

"It was just a tree," he explains.
"I'm not sure why it meant so much to me."
"Those were just stars," he says. "Is it so unfathomable
that constellations could be just negative paper space;
just light where the pen poked through?"

Atheism is a security blanket to him:
to me, blind faith is the last visible remainder
of light. The final rooted thing left to us; a climbable escape
from an incipient storm.

Once a fire, now a flood.

And Such Were Some of Us

This is the church,
this is the steeple,
open the doors and see all the people.

Here is the minister, saying his prayers;
here are the singers, going upstairs,

This is the wolf,
this is his lambskin,
keep your eyes closed and you won't see his sin;

here is the harlot, singing the hymn;
here are the angry, peaceful within.

This is the thief,
this is the liar,
no longer condemned; nor consumed by fire.

Here are the broken, pieced back together;
here are the doomed with hope of forever.

This is true love,
this is redemption.
This is forgiveness: utter exemption.

This is the church,
this is the steeple;
open the doors and see all the people.
This wolf on the back row;
this liar; this whore; our sins they are many-
God's mercy is more.

Après

(for T.C.L)

If you would have asked me what's leftover to say, now that August
has stranded me on the bridge, the compromise point
between Northshore and the Southside,
I would have likely said
"don't be a stranger"-

but what I would really prefer to mention is
that while the cicadas were chafing against the amber and cognac summer,
I was clearing out preserves of last year's bitterness and repurposing the
glasses to stockpile the same creek water
that was clotting the espresso hairs on the back of your forearms and
riling the pebbles to chuckle over the humorless Sunday afternoons.

I was screwing on capfuls of the same sunlight
that was tarnishing my shins to strawberry,
bleaching the home-going traffic lights the color of aperol spritz
and foreshadowing your body against the acid-washed sky-
the same sunlight that forgets its own strength on the virtue of its tenacity.

And I would love you in any summer. In any America. In any brutal
and transient thing worth striving to grasp-

but that's beside the point. Which is to say:
I was learning to store my own warmth
for the days when the sun pulls away.

Which is to say:
if you would have loved me, I would have felt it by now.

You've a head full of stars; I've the plans to sort them into constellations

Look,

not to be obtuse, but

fifth child to fifth child

I was never more than a handful of steps behind you.

And neither of us could afford to turn back

even though there were things in there worth saving. Worth living for.

We only knew it was dark matter

because of how our steps dragged as we passed through it.

It was what we made of it: we live with that, instead.

That Thanksgiving, something about the piano music pooling in the

dining room floor as we retraced art history taught me what it meant

to lead parallel lives with someone. To conjoin them. To tie them off

with one retraceable crimson thread.

To reunite a painting and a sculpture by the same artist, to compile them

in different collections of the unvarying museum they originated from;

to reconnect the dots between disparate maps; to pin them, overlapping,

to walls of homes we did not build but do not have to vacate;

to retell a myth without changing the meaning;

to charter odysseys into each other's orbits

again and again and again-

we binary stars with our gravitationally distorted vision

who leave the dream terrestrial.

Make of it what you will.

Is it trite? Am I too obvious for your subtleties?
Too heavy-handed with my galactic metaphors?
You are so understated that I sometimes feel that I am screaming in my
attempts to whisper.

Go on, bring me back down to earth. Tell me
obsession will spark from being the only two wildfire survivors
who can still run a finger through a tabletop candle flame
without flinching. I prefer to syncopate my circadian rhythms with the
footsteps marking off a trail of 'pleases' down the airport corridor,
mimicking the unbeatable rhythms
of your diplomatic heart.

It is only a love poem if you rewrite the ending.
It is what you make of it.

Headlines on Columbus Day

"Too much," my family says: "you ask for too much."
In this disposable wasteland,
insatiability will make an immigrant of your vagabond heart.

Because I want this
sliver of metal in the crosspiece of my palm to stop aching;

and this
worn charcoal mohair chair and this
heavy-eyed wonder
and this
peace treatise on a cafeteria napkin
and this
defaced clock sitting on its hands
and this
evening chamomile and this
reading news of a country that is no longer mine
to interpret the inflection of my motherland's tongue
without bearing the pain of her motherhood.

When the locals find my expatriated bones on a foreign coastline, they
will not mention that nothing from my country is built to last. Instead they
will say that they were good bones; that something
strong and safe must have been built around them:

"Where do you think they were going?"

That is what I want.

I want to stop renting the body that is my present address-
no more single-use existence, no more secondhand aspirations, no more
thinking twice about what is once in a lifetime, no more second thoughts
about first glances-
and they tell me I ask for too much.

I want this
discontent little America that I have discovered inside my own chest to
be my homeland, and not the sole place
I am exiled from-

and it is still
too much to ask.

No Goodbyes Left Unsaid

If the world was ending, imagine
the sun setting a final time on angry people who are forgetting to notice
the graceful movements of time, people
who are bloodthirsty for a sunrise that never comes: an entire city
of sleeplessness, an ecosystem of rage-

stop. That is not the ending we agreed on.

Before the curtain drops, we should have learned to stop rubbing skin off
the heels of our conversations
with attempts to walk miles in someone else's shoes,
bloodied by the irritating reminder of mindsets we've outgrown;
we should have stopped auditioning
for our own existences by now. We'll shrug off the hand-me-down anger-
sized for a lesser man- folding it around our resolve to outgrow it,
and tucking both into filing cabinets full of blueprints for diasporadic
backdrops we no longer have to construct. Nine moves in four years
before I finally felt at home in my own skin-
turns out nobody likes the body they grew up in, but you learn
to be proud of yourself for cooking instead of ashamed of yourself for
eating.

Were you praying for me yesterday, somebody?
Because for the first time in a long time, I felt sorry for something that
wasn't myself.

When the world is ending,
It will end like this. It will end
with the sudden small forgivenesses.
To a body.
To a stranger.
To a younger self.
To every god that has failed to merit your worship.

Let me be clear:
if there is no tomorrow, I will not waste what is left of today
on my own bitterness.

And End With a Hymn

Somedays   I fear
I am   being pitted against God
more poet than woman   the way the fruit I bear
more reason than rhyme   must rot on the tongue.

I plant nightshade   and he tends it, growing it
in my jaw   till it becomes an immunity;

and I am spell-bound   as   he   plots   constellations
dizzy, spinning;   across the graph of galaxies
some star-sailor   witness to the waltz of a universe
seasick on the dissolving planets   that he choreographed.

I open my mouth-   He smiles.
And it is empty.   And it is is fulfilled.
I open my hands   to grasp
completely   the mind of God-
it is all so out of reach,   unfathomable-
all this abandoning and   never forsaken,

this ceaseless wandering,

        no longer something to be mythologized:
                        for I am

                        rounding the corner of the labyrinth.

                                I am almost home.

52

author's note

"I had begun to compose myself."
- Natasha Trethewey, Memorial Drive

Having a father who was all at once a classicist, historian, and preacher leant itself to an abundance of religious texts on my childhood shelves- and I, black sheep that I am, was typically plunged into the depths of whatever mythological text he saw fit to populate said shelves with. (Needless to say, that early absorption has colored much of the metaphors and thematic elements found in this collection.) The rewritten version of the Æneid my father selected was titled "In Search Of a Homeland", by Dame Penelope Lively. I very much doubt she had any clue the title alone would be as formative as it has been to my internal self-mythologizing.

Every cultural mythology is a reflection of its place. My personal story- explored in the past three years and contextualized in these poems- is a reflection of my lack thereof.

From the age of thirteen on, I watched as one by one, everything calculated to keep me secure failed to do so. My home, my own body, my family, my church, my job, my school, my state, and eventually my country. I have endured the abuse of power, suicidal ideations, religious cover-ups, disordered eating, family crises, and a deep-set feeling of unease and displacement as I learned that this world was not my friend, and that every place I had relied on had crumbled. Structurally unsound from the very conception of the blueprint.

I am now verging on twenty-three – ten years too late to attend my own funeral. Ironically, I am now an interior designer: though I have striven and failed to find "home" for myself, my job is to create it for others.

But I do have the distinct advantage of being a poet- the ability to compose myself on these pages; to produce this in this volume a reconstruction of three formative years. Each of the sections has twelve poems, which roughly correlate with elements of the month they are ordered under. In 2022, (the nightshade) I was grieving the loss of my first love and my best friend, on the cusp of graduating college. I believed loyalty would save me. Bookended by two tragedies, 2023 (the labyrinth) found me grappling with my faith and my childhood experiences as I entered the professional world. I believed anger would save me. And in 2024 (the unraveling), I began unlearning bitterness and merging into a truer faith in God and my own perceptions- discovering a homeland that was accessible to me all along, from which I will never be excluded.

I have learned, by now, that forgiveness will save us all.

acknowledgments

Having my words dried out and preserved between these pages is largely owed to the following:

Aaron Quinn: without your encouragement and continual challenging influence, not a chance. I could not ask for a better publisher or more inspiring poet.

Mathaus Schwarzen: incredible friend, unbeatable critic, 'seraphic' editor- many thanks for the exceptional back cover summary and the very detailed (hilarious) critiques.

Tate Kiledjian: fellow empath and fabulous pre-reader.

Cara Cohn, who did it first.

Reece Gatlin, nee Carr: witness to my existence.

Dr. Daniel Gleason, who introduced me to received forms and the art of boxing.

Dr. Michael Palmer: purveyor of stories; whiskey in a teacup; a 'thin place'; the wisest person I know. You are the reason I continue my grapple with words.

Pierce St. Rose, for giving me the courage to make up terms like 'flimsical' and 'diasporadic'.

My four sisters.

My mother. (I do apologize for the singular profanity.)

The Wandering Poetry Circle- by extension, the 'poetry phone' collective. And for obvious reasons, Walnut Street Publishing.

www.ingramcontent.com/pod-product-compliance
Lightning Source LLC
Chambersburg PA
CBHW011218120626
46545CB00008B/3046